T0276074

BASIC JAVA PROGRAMMING

FOR KIDS AND BEGINNERS

GreatKnowledgesharing

Basic Java Programming for Kids and Beginners

iUniverse books may be ordered through booksellers or by contacting:

iUniverse
1663 Liberty Drive
Bloomington, IN 47403
www.iuniverse.com
1-800-Authors (1-800-288-4677)

ISBN: 978-1-5320-7875-0 (sc)
ISBN: 978-1-5320-7876-7 (e)

Library of Congress Control Number: 2019910175

Print information available on the last page.

iUniverse rev. date: 12/02/2019

Table of Contents

Intro

This book is written to help integrate children within the age of 11 and beginners alike into the art of computer programming using Java programming language. No prior knowledge is required in other to use this book. All the topics covered in this book utilizes a simple and easy to follow approach. There is a "do it yourself" exercise at the end of each lesson; these exercises give the readers an opportunity to apply what they've learned before proceeding to the next lesson. The exercises are written with a text editor in other to familiarize the readers with the basics of Java programming Language.

Why you should learn Java programming language:

Platform Independence: Java is one of the most dominant programming languages among the numerous programming languages that exist today. Java is a general-purpose high-level programming language and is commonly used for creating web and mobile applications. Java is designed to be easy to learn, write, debug, compile, and use. Java is also platform-independent, meaning Java can run on any hardware or software platform. The ability to run a Java program on any machine gives it an edge over other programming languages.

Employment Opportunities: Another reason to learn Java is because knowing how to program in Java, gives you an edge over others in terms of career growth and employment opportunities especially in this day and age where IoT (Internet of Things), AI (Artificial Intelligence) and Autonomous Driving are fast becoming the norm; making a good understanding of computer programming a must-have skill set. According to the United State Bureau of Statistics, employment of computer and information technology occupations is projected to grow 13 percent from 2016 to 2026, faster than the average for all occupations. These occupations are projected to add about 557,1000 new jobs. Knowing how to code (program) in Java will definitely put our kids and adult alike in an advantageous position.

Computer programming:

Computer programming is the art of writing a computer-executable code to accomplish a specific task.

Computer programming enables us to take control of a computer device. We tell the computer what to do by writing and installing an executable program that is executed by the computer upon request. Computer programming has evolved since inception, the reason for this evolvement, is the need to make programming language more user-friendly and powerful.

Computer Programming Language Generations:

Computer programming has gone through various stages of development, the first stage is known as the first-generation language, this was basic data instructions (machine language). Codes were written directly for computers to process; meaning there was no compilation of codes before execution. The second-generation language like assembly language uses an assembler to convert language statement into machine language. The third-generation language also known as the high-level language uses a compiler to convert the high-level language. Some examples of this are C, C++, Java, etc. The fourth-generation languages closely resembles human language. An example of this is the SQL programming language. The fifth-generation language uses a graphical interface to create a language statement.

History of The Java programming language:

The Java programming language is an object-oriented programming language (Programs that are organized around class, data, and objects) that was created by a small group of Sun Microsystem engineers known as the green tree in the early nineties. The team was led by James Gosling, Mike Sheridan, and Patrick Naughton.

JVM, JRE, and JDK:

The JVM (Java Virtual Machine) enables computers to run Java programs thus making Java platform independence. The JVM is part of the JRE (Java Runtime Environment). The JRE is the environment in which Java codes are executed. The JDK (Java Development Kit) is the package that contains both the JRE and JVM. You have to download the JDK in other for you to be able to develop a program in Java.

Java Programming Process Flow Diagram:

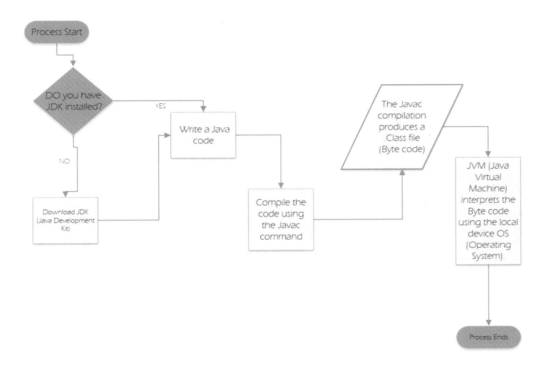

Java Programming Process Flow Diagram explained:

1. The first step begins with installing a JDK (Java Development Kit) on your system; if you don't have one already installed.

2. The second step is to write a Java code.

3. The third step is to compile the written code using the Javac command.

4. The output of the compiled code is a .class file (Byte code).

5. The final step is to run the compiled code on your local device. Your local device utilizes its internal JVM to interpret the byte code.

6. Process End

Chapter 1

Downloading and Installing Java JDK for Windows OS:

A Java Development Kit (JDK) is required in other for you to code and run a Java written program. The JDK is free for personal use and development work. You will need to agree to Oracle's license agreement before you can download it. Follow the steps outlined below to download and install a JDK. Please note that the installation steps outlined below are for Windows Operating Systems only. This book does not cover JDK installation for MAC OS.

1. Click on this link: JDK-URL to access Oracle JDK.

2. Click on the download button as highlighted in red.

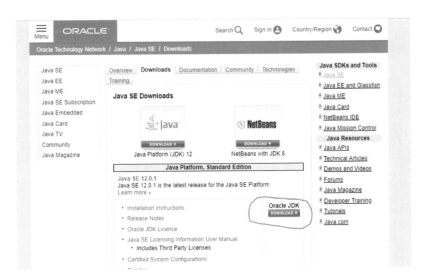

You need to accept Oracle license agreement in order to proceed. Please review the license agreement and click on accept license agreement radio button, and select the right product file for your computer as shown in the image below if you want to proceed with the installation.

See also:
- Java Developer Newsletter: From your Oracle account, select **Subscriptions**, expand **Technology**, and subscribe to **Java**.
- Java Developer Day hands-on workshops (free) and other events
- Java Magazine

JDK 12.0.1 checksum

Java SE Development Kit 12.0.1
You must accept the Oracle Technology Network License Agreement for Oracle Java SE to download this software.
○ Accept License Agreement   ⦿ Decline License Agreement

Product / File Description	File Size	Download
Linux	154.7 MB	jdk-12.0.1_linux-x64_bin.deb
Linux	162.54 MB	jdk-12.0.1_linux-x64_bin.rpm
Linux	181.18 MB	jdk-12.0.1_linux-x64_bin.tar.gz
macOS	173.4 MB	jdk-12.0.1_osx-x64_bin.dmg
macOS	173.7 MB	jdk-12.0.1_osx-x64_bin.tar.gz
Windows	158.49 MB	jdk-12.0.1_windows-x64_bin.exe
Windows	179.45 MB	jdk-12.0.1_windows-x64_bin.zip

3. Click next to continue with the download

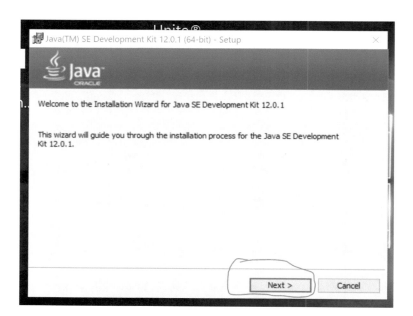

4. Click next to proceed if you are okay with the preselected install path for your Java development kit.

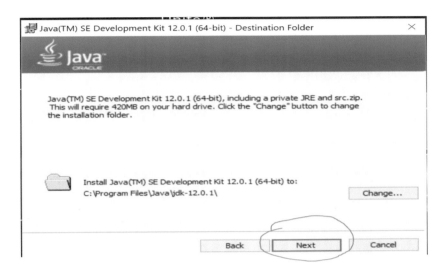

You should see a successfully installed message as shown below if everything goes well.

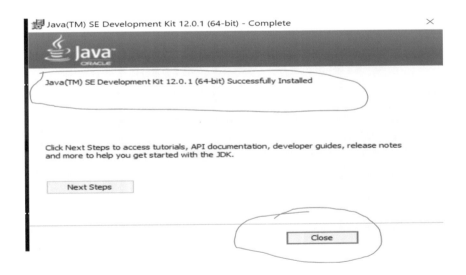

Congratulation, you have successfully downloaded and installed the JDK. Click on close to exit.

Setting up Environment Variables for Java:

Now that you have installed the JDK, the next step is for you to set up an environment variable, this will enable you to compile and execute your Java codes. What exactly are environment variables? Environment variables are global system variables accessible by all processes running under a particular operating system. Some examples of environment variables include User-name, Computer-name, System-root, etc.

You will need to step up an environment variable for your Java PATH. A PATH maintains a list of directories. Below are outlined steps for setting up an environmental variable:

1. Open up Control Panel on your computer, and click on System and Security.

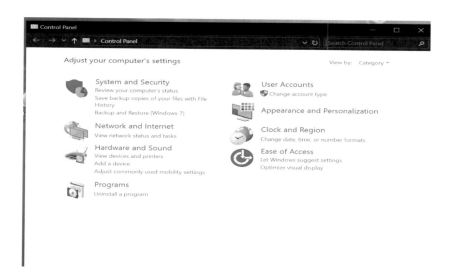

2. Click on System as highlighted below.

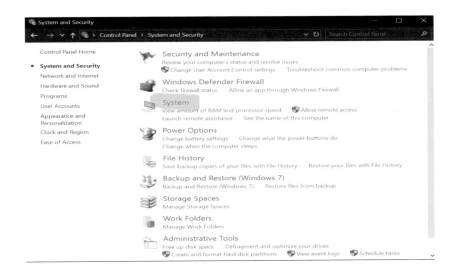

3. Click on Advanced system settings as shown in the image below.

4. Click on Environment Variables

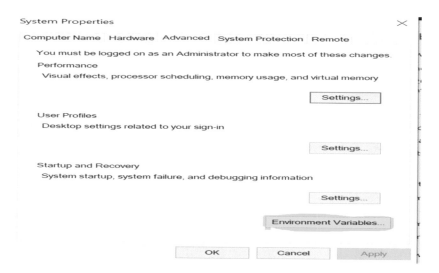

The next steps will require you to copy and paste the path where you have your Java/bin file into Path under System variables. Below are the steps on how to copy the Java/bin file path.

4a. Double click on the yellow folder icon (File Explorer) at the bottom of your computer screen.

4b. Click on Local Disk Drive C.

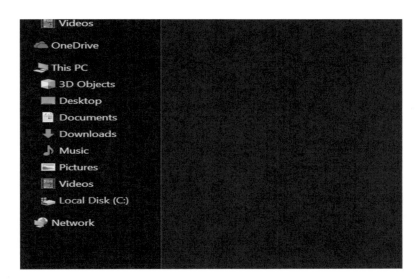

4c. Click on program files.

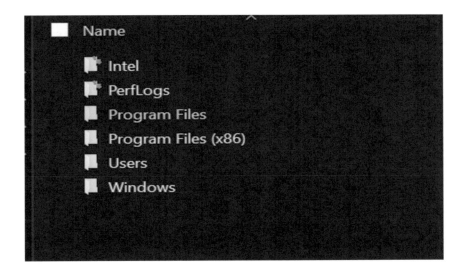

4d. Double click on Java.

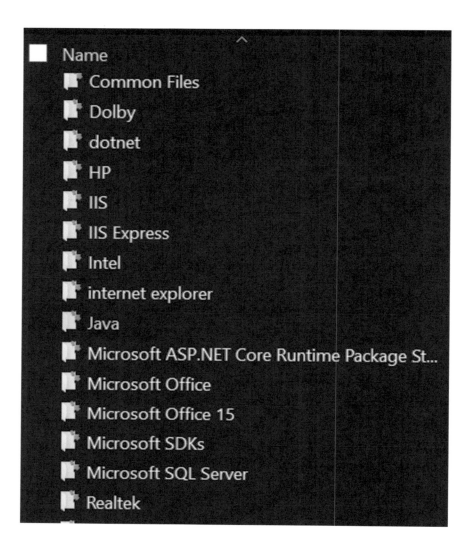

4e. Double click on JDK- "12" 12 is my JDK version as you can see below.

4f. Double on click bin.

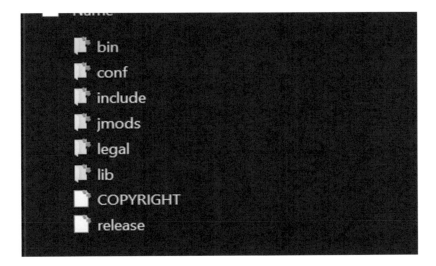

4g. Copy the path: This PC > Local Disk > Program Files >Java > JDK-12 > bin.

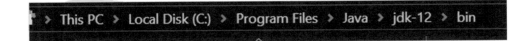

5. Locate "path" under System variables, highlight it as shown below and click on edit.

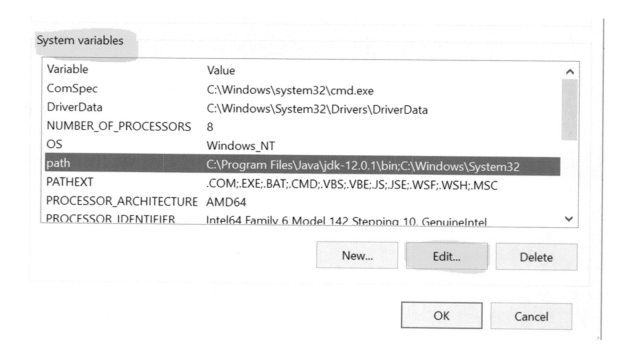

6. Click on new, and Paste the path that you copied in step 4g into the table. Click on ok.

7. Click on ok in the "System variable" window, and then click on ok in the "System Properties" window" to complete this step. Both the System variable window and the System properties window should already be open.

8. Open a command prompt window and type: "Javac" without the quotes as shown below:

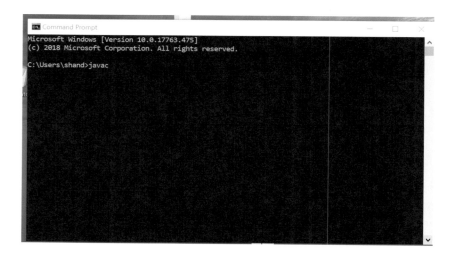

9. Press the enter key; your system should display the information as shown in the image below. If you don't see the image shown below, it means the environment variables were not set up correctly. You will have to repeat step 4g through 7.

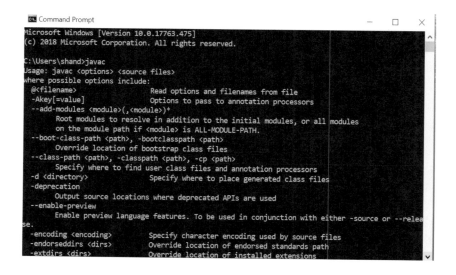

Chapter 2

The Qualities of a good programmer:

1. **Discipline:** A programmer ought to be disciplined. Programming requires a lot of focus and practice, without the aforementioned, it is practically impossible for anyone to grow in this field. Athletes and professional entertainers do not spring up overnight, they are expected to put in a lot of time into their training in other for them to become the best. The same thing applies to programming, the more time you put in the better you become.

2. **Patience:** This is another quality trait that a good programmer must possess, you are bound to run into challenges as you journey through the art of programming. There will come a time when you will feel like throwing in the towel (quitting) due to some coding-related challenges that you can't seem to find your way around. One thing to keep in mind is that in other for your program to work you have to abide by the set of rules that govern that particular programming language. These rules govern the way the computer responds to your written code. You will run into errors when you don't abide by these predefined set of rules. For example, a mistyped or misspelled word can create an annoying bug that has the tendency to hold you back for as long as that error exists.

3. **Practice:** The importance of practicing cannot be overemphasized. Practice they say makes perfect. There is no way you can grow if you don't practice. The more you practice the better you become and the more your confidence level grows. lack of practice will take you right back to where you started from.

4. **Comments:** get into the habit of commenting your codes, this will ensure continuity and eliminate a single point of failure from a business perspective. Comments make it easy for other programmers to pick up from where you left off.

Chapter 3

Your first Java program:

You've downloaded, and installed Java JDK, and have gone ahead to set up the environment variables. The next step is to write your very first Java program. That's right! Your very first Java program. So, let's dive into it.

HelloWorld! Program.

To write a program that displays HelloWorld on your computer screen you need to do the followings:

    1a. Right-click on your computer and click on "New".

    1b. Click on "Text Document" to open up a notepad as shown below.

1. Click on "file", and "Save AS" as shown below.

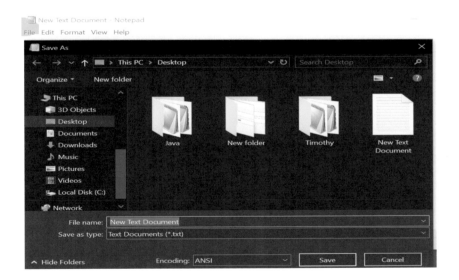

2. Enter HelloWorld.Java in the File name column as shown in the image below.

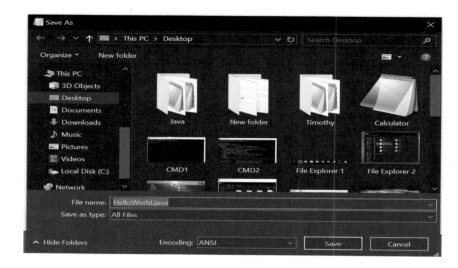

3. Select the location that you will like to store the file. I will suggest you create a new folder on your desktop, name the folder "MyFirstProject".

4. Select All Files as the "Save as type" and click on save.

5. Type the text below into the HelloWorld.Java notepad text file that you created (please do not copy and paste).

Programming Example #1

// My First java program

package helloworld;

class HelloWorld {

public static void main (String [] args) {

System.out.println("HelloWorld");

}

}

6. Save your file by clicking on >file>save.

7. Open a Command Prompt window, (CMD) you can do this by typing cmd in your computer search window.

8. Type: cd desktop and press the enter key.

9. Type: cd MyFirstProject and press the enter key.

10. Type: Javac HelloWorld.Java and press the enter key.

- You should see the image below if your program compiled successfully.

- The image below displays two files, one is a Java file that contains your code while the other one, is a Class file which contains your bytecode; this was generated when you compiled your code using the Javac command.

- If you received an error message, go back and retrace your step; you could have easily mistyped a word, omitted a step, or better still, you forgot to add a semicolon (;) or curly braces ({}).

- Please do not be too hard on yourself if you are unable to get it right after the first or second trial. This is expected. Keep trying until you get it right.

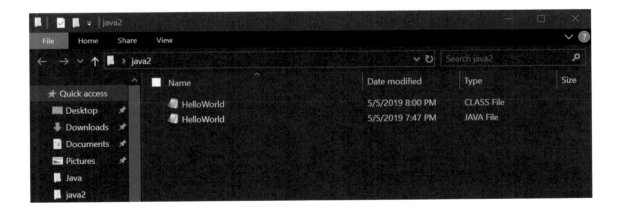

11. Type: Java HelloWorld.Java and press the enter key to run your program. You should see the image as shown below if your code ran successfully.

- The system executed your bytecode which is in the "class folder" when you typed: Java HelloWorld.java

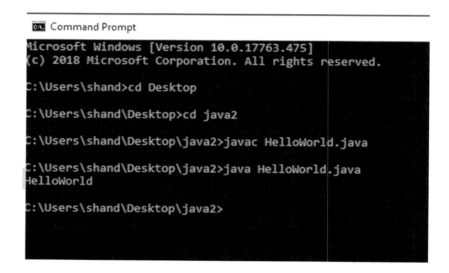

Congrats, you did it! You've successfully written your very first program in Java.

Explanation of the HelloWorld Syntax

The first thing that we did before we started writing our code was to write a comment that tells those that

have a business need to know what our code is all about: "// My First java program"

Comments: This can be written in either a single line (//) or multiline (/* */). The single-line comment// allows us to write a comment in a single-line, while the multiline comments allow us to write comments in multiple lines, for example, to use a multiline comment, type the following into your text editor between the forward-slash and asterisk and asterisk and forward-slash (/**/) in our HelloWorld code:

/* I am practicing how to

write a multiline code,

please bear with me.

*/

Save the file and run the file again. As you can see from the image shown below, the output of the code remained the same; that is to say, the comment that we added did not affect the execution of the code.

```
Command Prompt

Microsoft Windows [Version 10.0.17763.475]
(c) 2018 Microsoft Corporation. All rights reserved.

C:\Users\shand>cd Desktop

C:\Users\shand\Desktop>cd java2

C:\Users\shand\Desktop\java2>javac HelloWorld.java

C:\Users\shand\Desktop\java2>java HelloWorld.java
HelloWorld

C:\Users\shand\Desktop\java2>
```

Updated Code with a single line and multiline code:

Programming Example #2

```
// My First programming language

/* I am practicing how to

write a multiline code,

please bear with me.

*/

package helloworld;

class HelloWorld {

public static void main (String [] args) {

System.out.println ("HelloWorld");

}

}
```

Comments are not part of the code; they are neglected by the compiler when the codes are executed.

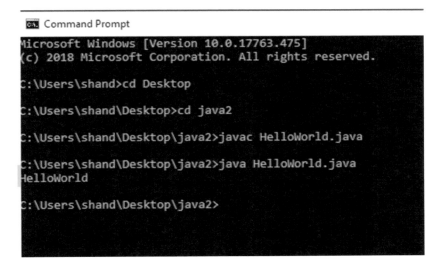

Our second line of code: "package helloworld;" tells the compiler to create a package called "helloworld" for us. This is where all the associated files for our code will be stored.

What is a package?

A package in Java can be defined as the grouping of related classes and interfaces. Programmers define a package at the beginning of their work; just like we did in our HelloWorld code. Package provides access protection and namespace management; that is to say, we can determine how related files can be accessed within our program, we can also prevent conflicts that result from using the same name within a program through the use of package. Package are declared using lower case to prevent conflicts with the related classes.

In our third line of code: "class HelloWorld" {, we declared a class known as "HelloWorld" at the end of it we inserted an open curly brace ({), the curly brace, are used to indicate the start of a code element in Java and some other programming languages. An important thing to note is that every open curly brace has an associated closing curly brace. Our code will not run if we fail to include a closing curly brace, rather we get a visit from our friend Mr. "error" whose job is to prevent us from moving forward until we adhere to the set of rules that govern the Java programming language.

What is a class?

A class can be defined as a category which contains data types, and methods. Within the class we have what is known as objects, we will discuss data type later in this book, but for now, understand that a class is a category which is made up of objects and it contains data types and methods.

Our fourth and fifth line of code: "public static void main (String [] args) {"System.out.println ("HelloWorld");

This is the code element of our program "HelloWorld" and it's known as the Main () Method. One key thing to note is that the main method is the entry point of the Java application. A method can be defined as a collection of statement that performs a defined task. When invoked, the method returns a value to the caller. You invoke a method by calling the name of the method. In our example, we called the method: println by declaring the class: System, which is a built-in class present in Java.lang package, and then: .out which a static member field (variable) of System class. We then proceeded by the invoking our method: println, this method prints the argument: HelloWorld to the console.

Public static void main (String [] args) explained:

Public: This is the access specifier meaning that methods written in other classes can access it. We do have other types of access specifiers such as protected, private, and default.

Static: This simply means that we can call the method using a class name without creating an object for it.

Void: This is the return type; in this case, we are saying return no value.

Main: The starting point of our program.

String [] args: This denotes the value that is passed to the main method.

The difference between System.out.println and System.out.print **method**

When we use "System.out.println" the console prints our argument on a separate line whereas with "System.out.print", the console prints our argument on the same line.

Modified "Hello World" code using a combination of one "System.out.println" and two "System.out.print."

As you can see from the image below the System.out.println resulted in our argument being displayed in one line whereas System.out.print resulted in our argument being displayed on the same line.

```
C:\Users\shand\Desktop\Java3>java HelloWorld.java
Hello World
Hello WorldHello World
C:\Users\shand\Desktop\Java3>
```

Do it yourself exercise 1:

1. Write a program that outputs your name and that of your friend on two separate lines.

2. Write a program that outputs your name and that of your friend on a single line.

Java Reserved Words:

Java, just like any other programming language has some reserved words that cannot be re-defined. The reserved words are known as keywords, and there 57 of them and 55 are in use. Below is the list of Java keywords:

abstract	continue	for	int	private	synchronized	WHILE
boolean	default	future	interface	protected	this	
break	do	generic	long	public	throw	
byte	double	goto	native	rest	throws	
case	else	if	new	return	transient	
catch	extends	implements	null	short	try	
char	final	import	operator	static	var	
class	finally,	inner	outer	super	void	
const	float	instanceof	package	switch	volatile	

Chapter 4

Variable

A variable is a reserved memory location. Variables are case sensitive, meaning; a and A; are not the same. A variable in Java can only contain letters, numbers, underscore, and $ sign. When naming a variable, the first letter of a variable cannot be a number, we declare a variable in Java by first defining the data type, and then we assign a name to the variable (i.e. a storage container for our data type). The data type is used by the operating system to determine the type of memory to allocate to the variable, the final step in this process is to assign a value to our variable.

Variable declaration example:

```
int a = 40;
```

In the above example, "int" is the data type, int stands for integer; we will cover this in details when we discuss datatypes. "a" is the variable name while "40" is the value that we assigned to our int datatype.

Java code example with int data type:

Programming Example #3

Method #1,

```
Package addition;

class Addition {

public static void main (String [] args) {

//My first addition using Java

int a = 40;

int b = 80;

int sum = a + b;

System.out.println(sum);



}

}
```

In the above code, we declared three variables: a, b, and sum with an int data type. The value for variable a is 40, while that of b is 80. To enable us to add the two variables we declared another variable called sum. We then used the + operator to add the two variables (a and b) together and used the System.out.println to display the value in our console

If you entered the code correctly, you should get the result below:

```
C:\Users\shand\Desktop\Java3>java Additon.java
120

C:\Users\shand\Desktop\Java3>
```

Our int can also be written in so many other ways, for example, we can declare our datatype and variables first and then assign a value to them on a separate line.

Programming Example #4

Method #2

Package addition;

class Addition1 {

public static void main (String [] args) {

//My first addition using Java

int a, b, sum;

a = 40;

b = 80;

int sum = a + b;

System.out.println(sum);

}

}

If you entered the code correctly, you should get the result shown below:

```
C:\Users\shand\Desktop\Java3>java Additon1.java
120

C:\Users\shand\Desktop\Java3>
```

Programming Example #5

Package addition;

class Addition2 {

public static void main (String [] args) {

//My first addition using Java

int a = 40, b = 80, sum = a + b;

System.out.println(sum);

}

}

If you entered the code correctly, you should get the result shown below:

```
C:\Users\shand\Desktop\Java3>java Addition2.java
120

C:\Users\shand\Desktop\Java3>
```

Types of variables in Java:

Local Variable: this type of variable is declared inside a method. They are created when a method is invoked. A local variable is only accessible inside the method.

Instance Variable: Instance variable is a variable that belongs to an object. This variable is created when an object is created and are accessible only to the creating object; they are destroyed when the object is destroyed.

Static Variable: This type of variable is also known as Class Variables, the static variable is similar to an instance variable, the only difference is that the static variable uses the "Static" keyword.

Do it yourself exercise 2:

1.

    I.   ) Declare 6 variable: A, B, C, D, E, and F.

    II.) Assign an "int" data type to your variables.

    III.) Assign the following values to your variables: A = 70, B = 90, C = 170, D = 80, E = 30 and D = 100. E) Add the values of these variables together using an additional variable called "sum", and express your answer using the "print" method.

    IV.) Using println method, instruct your console to print the following statement: "The addition of A, B, C, D, E, and F is" (the value of your variables added together)

2. Rewrite your program using the various methods that we covered in this lesson.

Chapter 5

Primitive Data Types:

When writing a program in Java, we have to first define the data type before we can assign a value to it. Java creates a space in memory based on the data type that we define; these data types are categorized as primitive data types. Below are the 8 primitive data types used in Java.

Data Type Name	Description	Size
int	int is a short word for integer, this data type store whole numbers from negative 2 to the 31st power to positive 2 to the 31st power	32 bit
byte	byte stores whole numbers from -128 to 127 (this type of data type is useful for saving memory in large arrays)	8 bit
short	short stores whole numbers from -32,768 to 32,767 (this type of data type is useful for saving memory in large arrays)	16 bit

Data Type Name	Description	Size
long	long store whole numbers from negative 2 to the 63rd power to positive 2 to the 63rd power (this is used when we need a range of value wider than those provided by int)	64 bit
Float	Float stores fractional numbers and should be used instead of a double if there is a need to memory in large arrays.	32 bit
double	double stores fractional numbers	64 bit
boolean	boolean store true or false values (this data type is used for tracking true/false conditions)	1 bit
char	char is a short word for character, it stores a single character (16 bit Unicode character)	16 bit

Java also provides support for character strings, enclosing a character string within a quote creates a String object.

Java code example with primitive data types:

Adding two whole numbers using int, byte, and shot:

Programming Example #6

Int data type example:

```
Package ad;

class inteee {

public static void main (String [] args) {

//Adding two whole numbers using the int data type

int a, b, c;

a = 4200;

b = 7000;

c = a + b;

System.out.println(c);


}


}
```

You should get the answer below if your code runs correctly.

```
C:\Users\shand\Desktop\Java3>java inteee.java
11200

C:\Users\shand\Desktop\Java3>
```

Remember that this data type stores whole numbers from negative 2 to the 31st power to positive 2 to the 31st power. Anything outside of this range will result in an error. See the image below:

```
C:\Users\shand\Desktop\Java3>java inteee.java
inteee.java:10: error: integer number too large
a = 8000000000;
    ^
1 error
error: compilation failed

C:\Users\shand\Desktop\Java3>
```

The above code resulted in an error because one of our values is outside the allowed range of negative 2 to 31st power to positive 2 to the 31st power.

Byte data type example:

To add two whole numbers using byte and short data types we will have to implement what is known as casting because byte and short data types do not support the + (operand). Casting enables us to promote the values to int values thus allowing us to add the two values together.

Programming Example #7

Package ad;

class byteee {

public static void main (String [] args) {

//Adding two whole numbers using the byte data type

byte a, b, c;

a = 28;

b = 8;

c = (byte) (a + b);

System.out.println(c);

You should get the answer shown below if your code runs correctly.

```
C:\Users\shand\Desktop\Java3>java byteee.java
36

C:\Users\shand\Desktop\Java3>
```

Below is an image of a code with a value (700) outside the allowable range: -128 to 127, As you can see, the code resulted in an error.

```
C:\Users\shand\Desktop\Java3>java byteee.java
byteee.java:10: error: incompatible types: possible lossy conversion from int to byte
b= 700;
    ^
1 error
error: compilation failed

C:\Users\shand\Desktop\Java3>
```

Programming Example #8

Short data type example:

```
Package ad;

class shortee {

public static void main (String [] args) {

//Adding two whole numbers using the short data type

short a, b, c;

a = 20000;

b = 10000;

c = (short) (a + b);

System.out.println(c);
```

You should get the answer shown below if your code runs correctly.

```
C:\Users\shand\Desktop\Java3>java shortee.java
30000

C:\Users\shand\Desktop\Java3>
```

The code below resulted in an error due to the value (50000) being outside the allowable range of -32768 to 32,767.

```
C:\Users\shand\Desktop\Java3>java shortee.java
shortee.java:9: error: incompatible types: possible lossy conversion from int to short
a = 50000;
    ^
1 error
error: compilation failed
```

Chapter 6

Basic Java Operators:

Java operators enable us to manipulate variables. For the purpose of this book, we will only cover the Arithmetic Operators, Relational Operators, Logical Operators, and Assignment Operators.

Arithmetic Operators:

Arithmetic operators are used for performing mathematical operations. Below is a list of arithmetic's operators in Java.

Operator	Description
Addition (+)	Use to add values together
Subtraction (-)	Use for subtraction
Division (/)	Use for division
Multiplication (*)	Use for multiplication
Modulus (%)	Use for division; returns a remainder.

Programming Example #9

Sample codes using Arithmetic's Operators.

```
//Sample code using arithmetics operators.

package arithmetics;
```

```java
class Arithmetics {

public static void main (String [] args) {int a = 180, b = 40, c = 70, d = 40;

//using the addition + operator

System.out.println (a + b);

//using the subtraction – operator

System.out.println (a - b);

//using the subtraction – operator

System.out.println (a - b);

//using the multiplication * operator

System.out.println (a * b);

//using the division / operator

System.out.println (a / b);

//using the modulo % operator

System.out.println (c % d);

}

}
```

You should get the answers shown below if your code runs correctly.

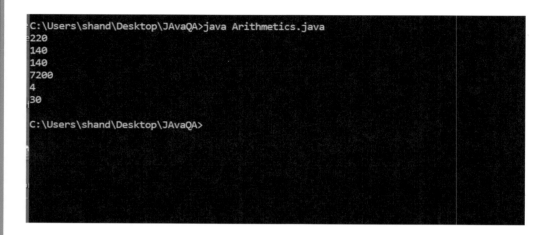

Sample codes using Arithmetic Operators Explained:

//using the addition + operator

System.out.println (a + b); This code returns a value of 220 that is (180 + 40)

//using the subtraction - operator

System.out.println (a - b); This code returns a value of 160 that is (180 – 40)

//using the multiplication * operator

System.out.println (a * b); This code returns a value of 7200 that is (180 * 40)

System.out.println (a / b); This code returns a value of 4 that is (180/40)

//using the modulo % operator

System.out.println (c % d); This code returns a value of 30 that is (180 % 40) Modulo returns the remainder of a division.

Do it yourself exercise 3:

1. Write a code that utilizes an int data type with the following values 200, 120, 50, 30, 60. to perform the following arithmetic operations: 1. Addition, 2. Subtraction, 3. Division, 4. Multiplication and 5. Modulo.

Relational Operators:

A relational operator is used to determine if there is a relationship between two data. Below is a list of relational operators in Java.

Operators	Meaning	Description
==	Equal to	This is used to affirm that the two values are equal.
!=	Not equal to	This is to signify that the two values are not equal.
Operators	Meaning	Description
>	Greater than	This is used to signify that the value on the left is greater than the value on the right.
>=	Greater than or equal to	This is used to signify that the value to the left is greater or equal to the value to the right.
<	Less than	This is used to signify that the value on the left is less than the value on the right.
<=	Less than or equal to	This is used to signify that the value on the left is less than or equal to the value on the right.

Programming Example #10

Sample codes using Relational operators:

//Sample code using equal to (=) relational operator

package relational;

class Relational {

public static void main (String [] args) {

int a = 80, b = 80;

//using the equal to operator

if (a == b)

System.out.println (" a is equal to b");

}

```
C:\Users\shand\Desktop\Java3>java Relational.java
 a is equal to b

C:\Users\shand\Desktop\Java3>
```
}

You should see the output shown below if your code runs correctly.

Programming Example #11

//Sample code using not equal (!=) relational operator.

package not;

class Not {

```java
public static void main (String [] args) {

int a = 70, b = 80;

//using the not equal to operator

if (a != b)

System.out.println (" a is not equal to b");

}

}
```

You should see the output shown below if your code runs correctly.

```
C:\Users\shand\Desktop\Java3>java Not.java
 a is not equal to b

C:\Users\shand\Desktop\Java3>
```

Programming Example #12

```java
//Sample code using greater than relational operators.

package greater;

class Greater {

public static void main (String [] args) {

int a = 90, b = 80;

//using the greater than operator
```

```
if (a > b)

System.out.println (" a is greater than b");

}

}
```

You should see the output shown below if your code runs correctly.

```
C:\Users\shand\Desktop\Java3>java Greater.java
 a is greater than b

C:\Users\shand\Desktop\Java3>
```

Programming Example #13

```
//Sample code using less than (<) relational operator.

package lq;

class Less {

public static void main (String [] args) {

int a = 60, b = 90;

//using the less than operator

if (a < b)

System.out.println (" a is less than b");
```

```
}


}
```

You should see the output shown below if your code runs correctly.

```
C:\Users\shand\Desktop\Java3>java Less.java
 a is less than  b

C:\Users\shand\Desktop\Java3>
```

Programming Example #14

//Sample code using greater than or equal to (> =) relational operator.

package gq;

class Greater {

public static void main (String [] args) {

int a = 90, b = 90;

//using the greater than or equal to operator

if (a > = b)

System.out.println (" a is greater than or equal to b");

}

}

You should see the output as shown below if your code runs correctly.

```
C:\Users\shand\Desktop\Java3>java GreaterQ.java
 a is greater than or equal to b

C:\Users\shand\Desktop\Java3>
```

Programming Example #15

//Sample code using Less than or equal to (< =) relational operator.

package lq;

class LessQ {

public static void main (String [] args) {

int a = 90, b = 90;

//using the less than or equal to operator

if (a <= b)

System.out.println (" a is less than or equal to b");

}

}

You should see the output shown below if your code runs correctly.

```
C:\Users\shand\Desktop\Java3>java LessQ.java
 a is less than or equal to b

C:\Users\shand\Desktop\Java3>
```

Do it yourself exercise 4:

1. Write a code that utilizes an int data type to compare the relationship of two values using the following relational operators: 1. Equal to, 2. Not equal to, 3. Greater than, 4. Less than, 5 Greater than or equal to, 7 Less than or equal to.

Assignment Operator:

An assignment operator is used to assign a value to a variable, for example, int a = 40. The "=" is the assignment operator; in this case, it was used to assign a value to variable "a" which has an int datatype. The assignment operator is not the same as the mathematical "=" (equal to) the symbol for equal to in Java programming language is "==".

Logical Operators:

The logical operators; also known as the Boolean logical operators are used to perform logical operations in Java; that is a condition-based decision. Below is the list of logical operators in Java programming language.

Operator	Name	Description
&&	Logical AND	The logical AND will only return a true value when both conditions are met.
||	Logical OR	The logical OR unlike the logical AND will return a value if one of the conditions are met and also when both conditions are true.

Operator	Name	Description
!	Logical Not	The logical NOT will return a true value when both conditions are false.

Programming Example #16

Sample codes using Logical Operators:

```
//Sample code the Logical AND (&&) operator

package logical;

class ABd {

public static void main (String [] args) {

int creditLoad = 120;

boolean courseCompletion = true;

if (creditLoad > 110 && courseCompletion) {

System.out.println (" He or she, is ready to graduate from college");

}

else {

System.out.println (" He or she, is not ready to graduate from college");

}

}

}
```

You should see the output shown below if your code runs correctly.

```
C:\Users\shand\Desktop\Java3>java ABd.java
 He or she, is ready to graduate from college

C:\Users\shand\Desktop\Java3>
```

The Logical && code explained

If you remember, in our previous lesson we talked about the condition that has to exist in other for our system to return a true value when we are dealing with logical AND (&&). The condition has to be true for the two values before our system can process our desired code. For the above code, the credit Load has to be above 110 and the course Completion has to be true in other for the student to be ready to graduate. If one of those conditions are not met, the system will return a "He or she, is not ready to graduate." Message. The code below depicts a situation where one the condition was not met.

Programming Example #17

//Sample code the Logical AND (&&) operator

package logical;

class ABd {

public static void main (String [] args) {

int creditLoad = 120;

```java
boolean courseCompletion = true;

if (creditLoad < 110 && courseCompletion) {

System.out.println (" He or she, is ready to graduate from college");

}

else {

System.out.println (" He or she, is not ready to graduate");

}

}

}
```

As shown in the image below, our code returned a false value due to the credit Load being below 110.

```
C:\Users\shand\Desktop\Java3>java AB.java
 He or she, is not ready to graduate

C:\Users\shand\Desktop\Java3>
```

Programming Example #18

//Sample code the Logical OR (||) operator

package logical;

```java
class Aor {

public static void main (String [] args) {

int creditLoad = 120;

boolean courseCompletion = true;

if (creditLoad > 110 || courseCompletion) {

System.out.println (" He or she, is ready to graduate from college");

}

else {

System.out.println (" He or she, is not ready to graduate from college");



}

}

}
```

For the logical OR (||) the system will return a true value on two conditions: 1, if both statements are true or if either one of them is true. The above code returned a true value because the requirements were met. That is, the credit Load is greater than 110 and the course Completion = true

```
C:\Users\shand\Desktop\Java3>java ABd.java
 He or she, is ready to graduate from college

C:\Users\shand\Desktop\Java3>
```

Programming Example #19

```java
//Sample code the Logical OR (||) operator

package logical;

class Aor {

public static void main (String [] args) {

int creditLoad = 120;

boolean courseCompletion = false;

if (creditLoad > 110 || courseCompletion) {

System.out.println (" He or she, is ready to graduate from college");

}

else {

System.out.println (" He or she, is not ready to graduate from college");


}

}

}
```

The above code returned a true value because one of the conditions is true.

```
C:\Users\shand\Desktop\Java3>java ABd.java
 He or she, is ready to graduate from college

C:\Users\shand\Desktop\Java3>
```

Programming Example #20

```java
//Sample code the Logical OR (||) operator

package logical;

class Aor {

public static void main (String [] args) {

int creditLoad = 120;

boolean courseCompletion = false;

if (creditLoad < 110 || courseCompletion) {

System.out.println (" He or she, is ready to graduate from college");

}

else {

System.out.println (" He or she, is not ready to graduate");

}

}

}
```

This time around, our code returned a false value because neither of the conditions is true.

```
C:\Users\shand\Desktop\Java3>java AB.java
 He or she, is not ready to graduate

C:\Users\shand\Desktop\Java3>
```

Programming Example #21

```java
//Sample code the Logical Not (!) operator

//Sample code using a Not (!) logical operator.

package logical;

class ABd {

public static void main (String [] args) {

boolean creditLoad = false;

boolean courseCompletion = false;

if (! creditLoad|courseCompletion) {

System.out.println (" He or she, is ready to graduate from college");

else {

System.out.println (" He or she, is not ready to graduate from college");

}

}
```

```
}
```

The above code returned a true value because both of the condition is false. The Not (!) logical operator is the opposite of the AND (&&) logical operator.

```
C:\Users\shand\Desktop\Java3>java ABd.java
 He or she, is ready to graduate from college

C:\Users\shand\Desktop\Java3>
```

Do it yourself exercise 5:

1. You have been asked by your teacher to explain the meaning of an AND (&&) OR (||) and NOT (!) logical operators to your class using any programing language of your choice. Going by what've learned from this lesson, right a simple program that returns a value that explains the meaning of the three logical operators when executed.

Chapter 7

Working with if-then, else-if, else, and switch statement in Java

The if-then and if-then-else Statements:

The if-then statement is used to tell our program to execute some part of our code when a given condition is met. The if-then statement can be used in conjunction with the other things that we have learned so far. A simple if-then statement can be written as follows:

Programming Example #22

```
//Sample if-then statement

package studentAge;

class StudentAge {

public static void main (String [] args) {

int age = 10;

if (age > 9)

System.out.println("The student is above 9 years old");

}

}
```

```
C:\Users\shand\Desktop\JAvaQA>java StudentAge.java
The student is above 9 years old

C:\Users\shand\Desktop\JAvaQA>
```

The above code is a simple if-then code that returns the value: "The student is above 9 years old" if the condition is met. The condition, in this case, is that the age of a student has to be greater than 9 (> 9) the if-then statement alone, is not enough to tell us everything that we will like to know. For example, if you ask someone to check to see if a friend of yours is inside the class and if he is, the person should notify you. This request is only useful if your friend is inside the class. What if your friend is not in the class? Remember that you did not add this scenario or condition to your request. Your condition is to check to see if your friend is inside the class. And if yes, return this value; "notify me")

Let us translate this into an if-then code:

Programming Example #23

//sample if-then statement

package friend;

class Friend {

public static void main (String [] args) {

boolean inTheClass = true;

if (inTheClass)

```
System.out.println("Notify me");

}


}
```

The above code returns the value "Notify me" as shown below when the condition is true. Which is great, what happens when the condition is false? In this case, you will get nothing back because you did not instruct your code to return a value if your friend is not in the class.

```
C:\Users\shand\Desktop\Java3>java Friend.java
Notify me

C:\Users\shand\Desktop\Java3>
```

The image below is the response that we will receive if our condition was to be false.

```
C:\Users\shand\Desktop\Java3>java StudentAge.java

C:\Users\shand\Desktop\Java3>
```

This is where the else statement comes in. The else statement enables us to return the desired value should the condition be false. See the example below with an if-then-else statement

Programming Example #24

```java
//sample if-then statement

package friend;

class Friend {

public static void main (String [] args) {

boolean inTheClass = false;

if (inTheClass)

System.out.println("Notify me");

else {

System.out.println (" He is not in the class");


}
}
}
```

The above code returns the value as shown below when the if condition returns a false value. (reprint)

```
C:\Users\shand\Desktop\JAvaQA>java Friendz.java
 He is not in the class

C:\Users\shand\Desktop\JAvaQA>
```

The Else if statement:

The else if statement is used in conjunction with the if and else statement in Java for conditional based decision-making purpose.

Programming Example #25

```
// Sample else-if statement



package elsee;



class Elsee {

public static void main (String [] args) {

int j = 50;

if (j < 20) {

System.out.println("The value is way too low");

}

else if (j <= 30) {

System.out.println("You are getting close");

}

else if (j <= 50) {
```

System.out.println("You got it, Congrats");

}

}

}

As you can see from the above code, the program that we wrote checks our code to see if there is any condition that matches the declared value, the program will execute that particular line of code once the condition is met. In this case, it printed the word "You got it congrats".

```
C:\Users\shand\Desktop\JAvaQA>java Elsee.java
You got it, Congrats

C:\Users\shand\Desktop\JAvaQA>
```

Switch Statement:

A switch statement allows us to test the condition of a variable against a list of values known as case. The switch statement works with a bunch of data types such as byte, short, char, int, etc.

The structure of a switch statement

Case: Case is used to hold value within a switch statement.

Break: A break is the termination point within a switch statement. That is the stopping point for our code, the code checks a particular case to see if a given condition is met, if yes, the switch breaks, if no, the code moves the next case and the cycle continues until it reaches the termination point.

Default: This returns a value when no condition is met. That is; the end of a switch statement.

Programming Example #26

Sample switch statement

```
/ /Sample switch statement

package month;

class WeekDays{

public static void main (String [] args) {

int day = 7;

switch (day)

{

case 1:

System.out.println("Perform Monday's task");

break;

case 2:

System.out.println("Perform Tuesday's task");

break;

case 3:

System.out.println("Perform Wednesday's task");

break;
```

```
case 4:

System.out.println("Perform Thursday's task");

break;

case 5:

System.out.println("Perform Friday's task");

break;

case 6:

System.out.println("Perform Friday night task");

break;

case 7:

System.out.println("Perform Saturday's task");

break;

case 8:

System.out.println("Perform Sunday's task");

break;




}


}


}
```

The above code will display the output below if typed correctly. We are simply instructing the system to display the case that aligns with the assigned int value which in this case is 7. The output below corresponds with case 7. Our system will return a different value every time we change the value of our int.

```
C:\Users\shand\Desktop\Java3>java WeekDays.java
Perform Saturday's task

C:\Users\shand\Desktop\Java3>
```

Our code will not return any value if we assign a value that is outside the range of our case.

In the example below, our code returned no value because the assigned int value is outside the case range of 1 to 8.

Programming Example #27

/ /Sample switch statement (with an out of range int)

package month;

class WeekDays{

public static void main (String [] args) {

int day = 10;

switch (day)

{

```java
case 1:

System.out.println("Perform Monday's task");

break;

case 2:

System.out.println("Perform Tuesday's task");

break;

case 3:

System.out.println("Perform Wednesday's task");

break;

case 4:

System.out.println("Perform Thursday's task");

break;

case 5:

System.out.println("Perform Friday's task");

break;

case 6:

System.out.println("Perform Friday night task");

break;

case 7:
```

```
System.out.println("Perform Saturday's task");

break;

case 8:

System.out.println("Perform Sunday's task");

break;



}


}


}
```

As you can see, our code returned no value because we assigned a value of 10 to out int

(integer).

```
C:\Users\shand\Desktop\Java3>java WeekDays.java
C:\Users\shand\Desktop\Java3>
```

To make our code return a value even when we are outside the range, we have to add "default" at the end of our code. The code below has "default" appended at the end.

Programming Example #28

```java
//Sample switch statement

package month;

class WeekDays {

public static void main (String [] args) {

int day = 10;

switch (day)

{

case 1:

System.out.println("Perform Monday's task");

break;

case 2:

System.out.println("Perform Tuesday's task");

break;

case 3:

System.out.println("Perform Wednesday's task");

break;

case 4:

System.out.println("Perform Thursday's task");
```

```
break;

case 5:

System.out.println("Perform Thursday's task");

break;

case 6:

System.out.println("Perform Friday's task");

break;

case 7:

System.out.println("Perform Saturday's task");

break;

case 8:

System.out.println("Perform Sunday's task");

break;


default:

System.out.println("You are out of range");

break;



}
```

```
}


}
```

Even though we are outside of our defined range of 1 to 8, adding "default" to our code enabled our code to return the value "You are out of range."

```
C:\Users\shand\Desktop\Java3>java WeekDays.java
You are out of range

C:\Users\shand\Desktop\Java3>
```

Do it yourself exercise 6:

Write a simple program that utilizes the if-then, if-then-else, else-if and switch statement.

Chapter 8

Loops in Java:

A loop can be defined as a piece of code that is continually repeated until a specified condition is met.

While Loop:

A while loop executes a line of code until a specified condition is met. The code will terminate once the desired condition is met, and when no condition is specified a While Loop can run infinitely.

While Loop Example:

Programming Example #29

```
//Sample while loop code

package k;

class Run {

public static void main (String [] args) {

int a = 0;
```

```
while (a < 10) {

System.out.println(" While loop example");

}

}

}
```

In the above code, we are simply telling our system to return the value "while loop example" if a < 10 (Less than 10) by invoking this method: System.out.println (" While loop example"); as you can see from our integer (int) declaration, the value of a is 0. Which is programmatically written like this: int a = 0; our code will run infinitely because of a < 10 (Less than 10). Below is the result of the above code.

To stop our while loop code from running infinitely, we will have to rewrite our code so that it increases its value by 1 each time it runs through the loop; this step will continue until our condition becomes false; that is, the condition that "a" is less than 10. Don't panic, this step will be done dynamically for us after we rewrite our code. Let's do it!!

Programming Example #30

```
//Sample while loop code with incremental value

package k;

class Run {

public static void main (String [] args) {

int a = 0;

while (a < 10) {

a++;

System.out.println(" While loop example");



}

System.out.println(" Hurray the loop is terminated");

}

}
```

Above is the updated code, I have included a++; to the code, a++; simply means: add 1 to the value of "a", remember that a = 0, the first time the code runs through the loop, the value of "a" = 0 will be presented, the second time it does that, the system will be presented with a new value: "a" = 1, this trend continues, until a becomes 10; at this point the condition (a < 10) will no longer hold; that is, it will become false. The code will terminate the moment the condition becomes false and print: "Hurray the loop is terminated". The first output shown below does not have "Hurray the loop is terminated" because we did not include the line of code: System.out.println(" Hurray the loop is terminated"); the second output has the word: "Hurray the loop is terminated" because we added System.out.println(" Hurray the loop is terminated"); to our code.

```
C:\Users\shand\Desktop\Java3>java Run.java
While loop example
While loop example
While loop example
While loop example
While loop example
While loop example
While loop example
While loop example
While loop example
While loop example

C:\Users\shand\Desktop\Java3>java Run.java
While loop example
While loop example
While loop example
While loop example
While loop example
While loop example
While loop example
While loop example
While loop example
While loop example
Hurray the loop is terminated
```

The for Loop:

This is another way to declare a Loop in Java, the difference between for Loop and while Loop, is that for Loop does not accept Boolean conditions but rather it takes 3 parameters: Initialization, condition, and value increment/decrement. Here is a sample for Loop code: for (int a = 0; a <10; a++). This line of code will generate the same result as that of while loop. The "int a = 0;" is the initializing aspect of the code; followed by the condition declaration: "0 < 10". The last part of the code is the increment: "a++" this once again, simply tells the system to add one to our assigned value. We could be written like this a--; that is to say, takeout 1 from our assigned value.

Programming Example #31

//Sample for loop code

package j;

class Jl{

```
public static void main (String [] args) {

for (int a = 0; a < 10; a++) {

System.out.println("for loop example");

}

System.out.println("for loop termination ends");

}

}
```

```
C:\Users\shand\Desktop\Java3>java J1.java
for loop example
for loop example
for loop example
for loop example
for loop example
for loop example
for loop example
for loop example
for loop example
for loop example
for loop termination

C:\Users\shand\Desktop\Java3>
```

The do while loop:

The do loop works by first executing the code before evaluating the condition. This is different from while loop and for loop which works by first evaluating the condition before executing the code.

Programming Example #32

Sample do while loop code

//do while loop example

```
package kg;

class Kg {

public static void main (String [] args) {

int a = 10;

do

{

System.out.println(«do while loop»);

}while (a < 10);

}

}
```

As you can see from the output below, our code returned a value even though the condition is false.

```
C:\Users\shand\Desktop\Java3>java Kg.java
do while loop

C:\Users\shand\Desktop\Java3>
```

Let's rewrite our code using a while loop and see what we come up with.

Programming Example #33

```
//while loop example

package kg;
```

```java
class Kgg {

public static void main (String [] args) {

int a = 10;

{

while (a < 10)

System.out.println(" while loop");

}

}

}
```

Our code did not return any value this time around because the value of a is not less than ten; making the condition false.

```
C:\Users\shand\Desktop\Java3>java Kgg.java

C:\Users\shand\Desktop\Java3>
```

Do it yourself exercise 7:

Write a simple program that shows the differences between while loop, for loop, and do while loop.

Chapter 9

Arrays:

An array is a variable that can store multiple values (elements) of the same data type at the same time using a method known as indexing (indexing is how Java stores array elements; 0 is the starting point of Java indexes). Array makes the job a programmer easier by allowing the programmer to assign multiple values to a variable. Below is how you declare an array.

Programming Example #34

```
//Sample array code

package game;

class Game {

public static void main (String [] args) {

int age [] = new int [4];

age [0]= 2;

age [1] = 4;

age [2] = 8;

age [3] = 16;
```

```
System.out.println (age [2]);




        }


        }
```

You should get the output that is shown below if your code runs correctly. The cool thing is that anytime you change the value of "age" in the System.out.println (age [2]) method, you will get a different output when you execute the code. For example, if you replace 2 with 3, and then run your code again, you should get 16 as your output because that is the value that we assigned to index 3.

```
C:\Users\shand\Desktop\Java3>java Game.java
8

C:\Users\shand\Desktop\Java3>
    ▮
```

Array code explained: To create our array, we started off by declaring our data type; in this case, we declared an int data type; the next step was to assign a variable (age) and then we inserted an open and close bracket [] which indicates that we want to create an array. "new int" this how we declare an object for our array; "[4]": this is the numbers of elements that we want our array to hold. For the array that we created, we assigned 4 as the numbers of elements; "age [2] = 8": this is how we assign a value to our elements; "System.out.println (age [2])": printed out a value of 8 which aligns with "age [2] = 8". Please remember to always start from 0 whenever you declare your indexes.

We can also create our array using this method: public static void main (String [] args) {

int age [] = {2,4,8,16}; and it will still return the same value. This method is a lot easier than the previous one.

Programming Example #35

```
//Sample array code

package gamz;

class Gamz {

public static void main (String [] args) {

int age [] = {2,4,8,16};




System.out.println (age [2]);


}

    .

}
```

```
C:\Users\shand\Desktop\Java3>java Gamz.java
8

C:\Users\shand\Desktop\Java3>
```

Strings:

Strings are a collection of characters and are used to store text. Strings are treated as an object in Java.

Programming Example #35

How to create a String

To create a String, we start off, by typing the word "String", we then declare a variable and then assigned a value to our variable.

Programming Example #36

```
//Sample String code

package kstring;

class Kstring{

public static void main (String [] args) {

String YourName = "Charles";

System.out.println(YourName);

}

}
```

You should get the output as shown below if your code runs correctly.

```
C:\Users\shand\Desktop\Java3>java Kstring.java
Charles

C:\Users\shand\Desktop\Java3>
```

Sample String code explained: in the above code we a declared a String variable: YourName, we then assigned a value to it: "Charles". Our system returned the value "Charles" when we invoke our method/class: System.out.println(YourName); We can also concatenate our code to return: "My name is Charles" by simply adding: "My name is " + YourName

Programming Example #37

```
//Sample String code

package kstring;

class Kstring {

public static void main (String [] args) {

String YourName = "Charles";

System.out.println("My name is " + YourName);

}

}
```

```
C:\Users\shand\Desktop\Java3>java Kstring.java
 My name is Charles

C:\Users\shand\Desktop\Java3>
```

as you can see the output of our code changed after we added "My Name is " + to our code. Always remember to add an extra space before the second quotation mark to avoid your output looking like the image shown below.

```
C:\Users\shand\Desktop\Java3>java Kstring.java
My name isCharles

C:\Users\shand\Desktop\Java3>
```

As you can see: "is" and "charles" are clustered together because we did not add an extra space between is and closing quotation mark (").

Do it yourself exercise 8:

Write a program that uses array to store 20 values. Use the two methods discussed in this lesson.

Chapter 10

Scanner Class:

Scanner class is used to obtain inputs of the primitive data types and etc. in Java. To create a Scanner class, we start off by importing the Java.util package; not doing so will result in an error when we run our code.

Sample Scanner Class Exercise

For this exercise, we will develop a simple calculator that adds two number together using the int data type. We will use a Scanner class to get user input.

Programming Example #38

Code for our simple calculator:

```
import Java.util.Scanner;

//Simple Scanner code

class Ysc{

public static void main (String [] args) {

Scanner addition = new Scanner (System.in);
```

```
System.out.println("Addition Calculator. Please enter a number");

int number1 = addition.nextInt();

System.out.println("Thanks! Now enter a second number");

int number2 = addition.nextInt();

int c = number1 + number2;

System.out.println("The sum of the two numbers is: " + c);

}


}
```

If you entered the code correctly and you used 560 and 740 as the two int values, you should see the answer shown below

```
C:\Users\shand\Desktop\Java3>java Ysc.java
Addition Calculator. Please enter a number
560
Thanks! Now enter a second number
740
The sum of the two numbers is: 1300

C:\Users\shand\Desktop\Java3>
```

The addition Calculator code explained:

The first thing we did was to import Java.util.Scanner; this is one of the inbuilt Java class. The second thing that we did was to write a code that utilizes the imported class to perform the arithmetic calculation. The key thing to remember is that Java.util.Scanner enables us to obtain inputs from the users through the keyboard. This is the only reason why are using it. The addition is done using what we've covered in our previous lessons.

Scanner addition: This is how you tell Java that you want to invoke the scanner class; addition: is the name we assigned to the object of the class.

= new Scanner (System.in): This is how you tell the system that you to want to take users input.

System.out.println("Addition Calculator. Please enter a number"); This enables you to get user's input from the keyboard.

int number1 = addition. nextInt (); This is a place holder for the user input, you will need to do this for all the inputs that you intend to collect from the users.

System.out.println("Thanks! Now enter a second number");This enables us to collect the second input from the user; int number2 = addition. nextInt (); This is a place holder for the second user input.

int c = number1 + number2; This enables us to perform addition using the addition (+) operator.

System.out.println("The sum of the two numbers is: " + c); This is how we print the output to the console.

Jar File:

A jar (Java archive) file enables us to package Java files for archiving, easy distribution, and execution.

Some JAR Files Commands and Meaning:

Command	Function	Notes
Jar cf (filename with .jar extension) input files for example: jar cf az.jar Age. class	To create a jar file.	C: stands for create F: stands file
Jar tf jar-file	To view the contents of the jar file.	T: stands table of content F: stands for file (jar file content)
Jar xf jar-file	To extract the contents of a jar file.	X: stands for extraction F: stands for file
Jar uf jar-file input files	To updating a jar file	U: stands for update F: stands for file
Jar cmf jar-file existing manifest.txt input-files. For example: jar cfm az.jar Age. class	This enables us to include manifest information from a different manifest file.	C: stands for create F: stands file M: manifest

Jar File Creation Step:

1. Create a text file and name it "manifest.txt"

2. Open the created text file and type the following: Main-Class: "Your class name". For example, Main-Class Ysc. Click the enter key twice, and close the file.

3. Compile your Java program file Using the Javac command on a command prompt window as shown below:

```
C:\Users\shand\Desktop\Addition>javac Ysc.java

C:\Users\shand\Desktop\Addition>
```

4. The Javac command will generate the class file, see the image below

5. Copy and paste the manifest.txt file into the folder containing the class and Java file.

6. Open a command prompt

7. Navigate to the folder location where you have your files:

8. Type the following in the command prompt window: Jar cfm jar-file.jar manifest.txt input-files. You can name your "jar.file.jar" whatever you want; type the word manifest.txt and add the associated files; in this case, we will add our class file (Ysc). Here is an example: "jar cfm AdditionCalculator.jar manifest.txt Ysc.class".

9. Click the enter key.

- You should see the jar file in the location where you saved your Java files. See the sample image below.

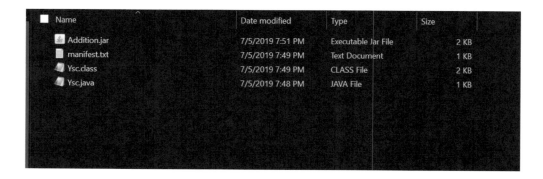

- Congratulation! You've just created your first jar file.

The META-INF subfolder is part of the files that Java created for you and it is stored inside your jar file. This file contains your manifest txt file. To extract the META-INF file from our jar file; do the following: Open the command prompt and navigate the folder location where you have your files and type the following: jar xf AdditionCalculator.jar. This will generate the META-INF file as shown in the above image. Double click on the file and click on manifest.txt You should see something like this: Main-Class: Ysc. Ysc is the name of my class so yours might be different. See the sample images below:

MANIFEST - Notepad

File Edit Format View Help

Manifest-Version: 1.0
Main-Class: Ysc
Created-By: 12.0.1 (Oracle Corporation)

How to Test your Jar file:

Now that you have built your Jar file, the next step is for you to test it. To do this; open the command prompt window, navigate to the folder location where you stored your Java files; and type the following: Java –jar Addition.jar. click the enter key and type any int value of your choice to perform a simple addition. If everything works correctly you should see the following:

```
C:\Users\shand\Desktop>cd FRiday

C:\Users\shand\Desktop\FRiday>java -jar Addition.jar
Addition Calculator. Please enter a number
4
Thanks! Now enter a second number
6
The sum of the two numbers is: 10

C:\Users\shand\Desktop\FRiday>
```

The above image indicates that your jar file is working as expected. Congrats! You are now able to run your program on any computer. To make it easier for you to run your jar file, you will need to create a bat (batch) file. A bat file enables us to run our jar file without opening a command prompt. To create a bat (batch) file do the following:

1. Open new a text editor and name it Run.bat.

2. Open the newly created bat file and type in the following: Java –jar "your jar file name with the .jar extension) in our case we will type the following: Java –jar Addition.jar

3. The bat and jar file must be stored in the same location in other for your bat file to run. Double click on your bat file to open up your program.

You should see the following if your bat file ran successfully

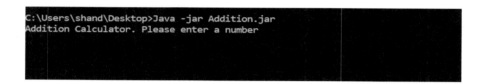

To prevent your jar file from closing when you enter your second input; enter the following line of code at the end of the simple scanner code:

Scanner mike = new Scanner (System.in);

mike.nextLine();

You will need to create another jar file in other to incorporate your changes. Run the code using the addition. bat that you created; your program should work as expected now.

Do it yourself exercise 9:

Develop a basic calculator that takes two input from the user to perform the following arithmetic operations: Addition, Subtraction, and Division.

Develop a program that takes 3 inputs from the user to divulge some information about them.

Develop a simple scanner calculator that is capable of performing a multiplication operation.

Chapter 11

Java Random Class:

Java random class is part of Java.util Package Classes. Java Random class is used to generate a stream of pseudorandom; also known as deterministic random bit generator.

Sample code with Java Random class

Programming Example #39

```java
import java.util.Random;

//Sample random code

class Jet{

public static void main (String [] args) {

Random clip = new Random ();

int number;

for (int counter =1; counter<=10; counter++) {

number = 1+clip.nextInt(10);

System.out.println(number + " ");
```

```
}


}


}
```

The image below is the output from the above code, as you can see, the numbers change every time you run the code. This is what randomization is all about.

```
Microsoft Windows [Version 10.0.17763.557]
(c) 2018 Microsoft Corporation. All rights reserved.

C:\Users\shand\Desktop>cd JetRandomization

C:\Users\shand\Desktop\JetRandomization>java Jet.java
9
3
9
4
8
3
4
5
8
1

C:\Users\shand\Desktop\JetRandomization>java Jet.java
10
8
6
1
10
2
5
2
5
7

C:\Users\shand\Desktop\JetRandomization>
```

Sample random code explained:

To generate our random code, we started off, by importing java.util.Random which is part of the Java inbuilt classes. We then follow the normal coding process. Random clip = new Random (); (this is how you create an object for your class)

int number; (we declared a primitive data type: int and assigned a variable named: number to it)

for (int counter =1; counter <=10; counter++) {(we are simply using a for Loop to telling the system to add to 1 counter = 1 until it reaches 10. Remember that ++ is the way that we tell the system to increment by 1 every time our code runs)

number = 1+clip.nextInt(10); (We added 1 before are clip object in other to prevent 0's from showing up in our results, had we not done this, we will have zeros in our outputs)

System.out.println(number + " "); (This is how we generate the output)

Do it yourself exercise 10:

Use your knowledge of Random and Scanner class to develop a simple program that gives the users 10 options to choose from; after which the program randomly chooses a number from the 10 options and declares it as a winner.

Chapter 12

Simple GUI Using JOptionPane

GUI stands for graphical user interface, so far everything that we've done till now has been command prompt base, which is very good for beginners as it allows you to know what is going on behind the scene until you are ready to start working with IDE's. IDE stands for Integrated Development Environment. IDE's makes programming a lot easier assuming you understand the basic concept; which is why we started off with the good old text editor.

For this exercise, we are going to utilize a Javax.swing.JOptionPane; this is an in-built class that stores all the component that we need. Below is a sample code that utilizes JOptionPane class:

Programming Example #40

```
//Sample Java GUI exercise


import javax.swing.JOptionPane;

//Sample Java GUI Excercise code

class GUII{

public static void main (String [] args){
```

```
String fn = JOptionPane.showInputDialog(" Prince & Princess Basic Addition Calculator: Please enter a
number");

String sn = JOptionPane.showInputDialog("Thanks! Now enter a second number");

int num1 = Integer.parseInt(fn);

int num2 = Integer.parseInt(sn);

int sum = num1 + num2;

JOptionPane.showMessageDialog(null, "The answer is: " + sum, "Basic Addition Calculator", JOptionPane.
PLAIN_MESSAGE);



    }


    }
```

Sample Java GUI exercise explained

The first thing we did was to import the javax.swing.JOptionPane after which we followed our standard coding practice until we got to the new introductions: String fn = JOptionPane.showInputDialog. We created a String variable called fn (first number) and sn (second number) after which we called the JOptionPane class and the ShowInputDialog method to enable us to take string inputs from a user and store it in our fn and sn variables. Since we are only capable of inputting String into our "ShowInputDialog" box we have to come up with a means to convert our String input into an integer. To do this, we use the: int num1 = Integer. parseInt(fn); and int num2 = Integer.parseInt(sn); what this does is that, it allows us to convert the value of variable fn into that of int num1 and the value of variable sn into int num2 and from there we are able to do our basic addition using int sum = num1 + num2. To display our answer, we use the showMessageDialog method. Here is how we invoked that method: JOptionPane.showMessageDialog. This method accepts four parameters: "null" this enables **us to center** our GUI, the second parameter allows us to display a comment, the third one, enables us to add a title to our GUI, and the forth one, enables us to decide how we want our message to be displayed.

If you entered the code correctly, you should see the images below when you run your program. I went ahead and created a jar file for our program. You can double click on the jar file after creating it to run the program. You don't need to create a bat file for this exercise since we are working with Java GUI.

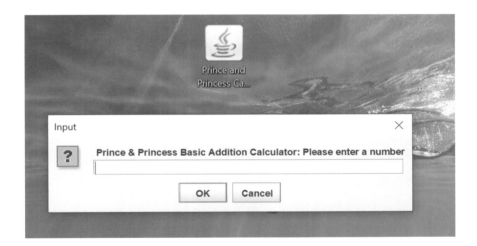

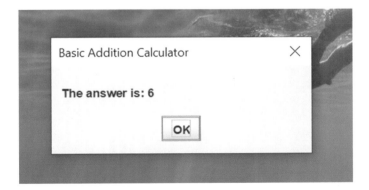

The addition result:

Do it yourself exercise 11:

Using the JOptionPane, develop a basic calculator that performs a multiplication operation.

Bonus Exercise:

Programming Example #41

Simple Head or Tail Game:

import java.util.Random;

import java.util.Scanner;

      class Gaming{

      public static void main(String[] args){

Scanner addition = new Scanner (System.in);

System.out.println("Welcome to the Head or Tail Game!");

System.out.println("Game rules: You need two people in other play this game");

System.out.println("Pick a side (head or tail) ");

System.out.println("Press any number to start the game.");

```java
int number1 = addition.nextInt();


        Random face = new Random();

        int headTail = 1 + face.nextInt(2);

        switch(headTail){


        case 1:

        System.out.println("HEAD it is");

        System.out.println(«Congrats! Press the pgUp key and hit enter to play again ");

        break;


        default:

        System.out.println("TAIL it is");

        System.out.println("Congrats! Press the pgUp key and hit enter to play again");



        }

        }

}
```

In the above code, we used a combination of Java Random, and Scanner in-built class and a switch statement. Go over the code and read through it line by line, if you run into any problem revisit the section in the book that covers the methods applied to develop this program.

The above code if entered correctly will generate the image below:

```
(c) 2018 Microsoft Corporation. All rights reserved.

C:\Users\shand>cd Desktop

C:\Users\shand\Desktop>java Gaming.java
Welcome to the Head or Tail Game!
Game rules: You need two people in other play this game
Pick a side (head or tail)
Press any number to start the game.
9
HEAD it is
Congrats! Press the pgUp key and hit enter to play again

C:\Users\shand\Desktop>
```

```
C:\Users\shand\Desktop>java Gaming.java
Welcome to the Head or Tail Game!
Game rules: You need two people in other play this game
Pick a side (head or tail)
Press any number to start the game.
8
TAIL it is
Congrats! Press the pgUp key and hit enter to play again

C:\Users\shand\Desktop>
```

Programing Development Steps:

The first thing that you need to do before you write a program is to brainstorm your ideas. Once you are satisfied with your ideas; you can then move on to the next phase which is documentation. Include a detailed plan on how you intend to implement your ideas in your document. Once you complete the documentation phase, the next step is to develop a prototype or a POC (Prove of Concept). The purpose of a POC is to ensure that your program will work as intended. once you are satisfied with your POC, you can now move on to the final phase which is development, testing and deployment.

Fun Practice Exercises:

We are going to apply everything that we've learned so far to build some very cool programs. These exercises will enable you to put your knowledge to test, it will also challenge you to start thinking like a programmer. Remember, the only way to grow your programming skill is through practice. Let's get started.

Project 1:

A friend of yours who heard that you are learning how to program in Java reached to you for assistance with his homework. His homework assignment has to do with writing a program in Java that is capable of taking 2 inputs from users to perform the following arithmetic operations: Addition, Subtraction, Division, and Multiplication.

1. Write a Java program that satisfies your friend's request.
2. Create a jar and bat file for the program.

Project 2:

You and your family are visiting your grandparents for a family get together; your grandma approached you because she heard that you are now a Java program protégé, she requested that you showcase your programming skills to your extended family by developing a game that everyone can participate in. Going by what you've learned so far; develop a simple guessing game that provides users with four choices.

- Hints: You will need a Java Random, and Scanner class for this project.

- Ensure to create a jar file for your guessing project.

Project 3:

Design a basic calculator that takes 2 inputs from a user to perform the following operations: 1, additions, 2, subtractions, 3, multiplications and 4, division.

Project 4:

Design a basic calculator that is capable of performing a multiplication operation using the Javax JOptionPane class.

Project 5:

Develop a program that can perform randomization using two values e.g. A or B, High or Low, etc.

Project 6:

Develop a car guessing game that gives users 10 option to choose from.

Answers to all the "Do it yourself exercises" and projects can be found in:
www.greatknowledgesharing.com

Printed in the United States
By Bookmasters